THE ASPECTS OF A VIRTUOUS *Woman*

THE ASPECTS OF A VIRTUOUS Woman

SONIA WILLIAMS

THE ASPECTS OF A VIRTUOUS WOMAN

iUniverse books may be ordered through booksellers or by contacting:

iUniverse
1663 Liberty Drive
Bloomington, IN 47403
www.iuniverse.com
1-800-Authors (1-800-288-4677)

ISBN: 978-1-5320-0430-8 (sc)
ISBN: 978-1-5320-0431-5 (e)

Library of Congress Control Number: 2016912710

Print information available on the last page.

iUniverse rev. date: 08/04/2016

Foreword

Our relationship began over 20 years ago when I served as your college pastor during your college days at the University of Southern Mississippi. From the days of weekly, campus Bible studies, to our Bible study group visiting your hometown and meeting your family, to the present where I enjoy partnering with you in local ministry, I find myself watching you, as an adult, handle the highs and lows of life that adulthood presents. God has used the pressures and trials of your personal life experiences, to form virtue in you! It's no surprise that this would be such an important topic for you to begin your writing experience.

The Bible reminds us of how valuable and precious virtuous women are and I pray that as women share your personal, written account in this book, they will allow God to unmask and bring to life the virtue that He has placed in all of them! May each reader approach this reading with the same openness and humility you had as a growing and learning believer on the USM campus decades ago...and God is certain to enlighten more and more!

Pastor Robert Johnson

Chapter 1

"DAUGHTER'S PERSPECTIVE"

To begin this book, I wanted my daughter to read and study Proverbs 31 and to expound on what she learned from her study. The following is what she wrote from her studies:

A wife with a good heart, humble attitude, and loving character is worth more than all the money in the world. Her husband is not ashamed of her. She helps him through his problems instead of trying to set him up. She's devoted to her husband and is willing to do anything for him (within reason). She always works hard and late to make sure he has what he and her family needs. She is kind-hearted, confident, and generous to people and it shews in her character. She's not spiteful or ill-minded, but she smiles and laughs with the world. She is a good Christian and always will be. She never plots against people, but helps them when they need it most. She offers encouragement to others. She cooks and cleans for her husband, family, servants, and other people. She has a strong will and a brave heart. She does not let her beauty or success go to her head, but reminds herself that she is no better or worse than anyone. She always does what God tells her to do. She knows where her priorities need to be. She knows what to say and how to say something to someone. She teaches people about the goodness of God and shares her stories. Everyone loves how her attitude inspires other to do better. Men flirt and try to catch her eye, but she only has eyes for her husband. She works for what she wants and earns what she gets.

Chapter 2

WHAT DOES IT MEAN TO BE VIRTUOUS

As I began this study of being a virtuous woman, I found there was so much to learn in becoming the virtuous woman God has created me to be. This particular subject is dear to me because I wanted to know what God really thought of me. I grew up in a house of mostly women. For a long time, the only male in the house was my teenage cousin. My mom gave birth to my brother when I was 10 and my second brother when I was 12, so that still left a house full of women. I had the responsibility of helping take care of my brothers. My grandmother and mother raised me to be self-sufficient. I knew how to cook, clean, change a tire, change oil, and many other things that would be considered a duel role.

When I left for college I took that same mentality with me. I didn't need anyone to help me do anything. I could do it myself or figure out a way to do it. It carried over into my relationships. A guy would try to buy or do things for me, but I made it so difficult and would not allow him to be the man that he was trying to be in my life. After a few failed relationships, failed friendships, and a failed marriage I began to ask God if something was wrong with me. I began to alienate myself from friends and became a loner. I only talked to my family because they were the only ones I felt I could trust to be me. I began to doubt who I was and who I was called to be.

I took a look at my failed marriage and began to see where my dominate personality showed. There were many issues with my marriage but during the last 2 years, I began to work on being the *perfect* wife. I began to ask his opinion and thoughts regarding decision-making for the home in an attempt to allow him to be the head of the house. In reality, I realized that I was the final decision maker in most instances. This had gone on for so long that I began to see that he didn't know how to be the man of the house. With all of the many issues we had, things began to go from bad to worse in a matter of months. The marriage ended after 10 years.

I began dating after the divorce and I started seeing a pattern of men I would attract. They would be those who were not looking for a commitment. Men would say that they were looking for a committed relationship, but I would later find that had were dating another female or not really wanting to commit. I would also have those who would say upfront they only thing they were looking for where one night stands. I began to ask God what was really going on with me and why I only attracted men who had no intentions of ever committing to me. I began to tell God the type of man I wanted and I was very specific. I wanted a man who was taller than 6'3". He had to love God first and foremost, have a steady job, love his family, love my daughter, and treat me the way God intended for me to be treated. My primary prayer began to be that God worked on me and that I may be the woman he intended for me to be. I also prayed that I would realize the true value of my worth. I began to see I couldn't be the friend, family member, or wife that God called me to be without truly knowing how He actually felt about me.

As I began seeking God, my study took me to Proverbs 31 where it discussed the different attributes of a virtuous woman. What made this study so very interesting is that, I began to listen more and more to the women around me and what their desires in life were as it pertained to finding a mate. In addition to that I realized more and more women were talking about waiting on their "Boaz" to find them. In seeing and hearing those comments I had a few thoughts. "Why does God wait so long to send women their mate?" Is it the woman? Is it the man? Could it be a combination of both? Those were some of the questions I wanted answered as I studied how God viewed a virtuous woman.

When I really began reading Proverbs 31 to get a full understanding, I took the scriptures in a literal context and spent my time thinking I had to do precisely as the scripture said. I questioned God and wondered if I could possibly become this virtuous woman He was talking about in scriptures. I could not do half of the things listed, i.e. verse 19 "she layeth her hands to the spindle, and her hands hold the distaff" (KJV). God had to take me out of my analytical train of thoughts and show me how the scriptures took on a totally different nature and meaning. I began to see that it did not mean 'spindle' in the literal sense. It meant that she was a hard worker and did what was needed to make sure her home was well taken care of. God gave me a whole new meaning of the scriptures. As I take you through my journey of finding answers to my questions, I pray you will see and be encouraged by what I have studied and learned about the many different women of the bible who God considered to be virtuous. I sincerely pray that you learned as much, if not more, about being the virtuous woman that God has called all women to be.

I have spoken with women on many occasions and asked the question, "Do you really know your worth?" A woman's worth simply means knowing what God thinks of you verses what you think of yourself. It took me some time to completely comprehend that God loves me no matter what. In spite of all my faults, failures, and horrible judgmental decisions; God still sees me as the apple of His eye. That fact that I am the apple of His eye is so awesome to me because shows in the life of Jesus. As you follow the life of Jesus, you will notice that He never disrespected a woman. He was always there to uplift, comfort, heal, and deliver women no matter the situation. An example of this kind of love is when Jesus met the Samaritan woman at the well. He didn't treat her like she was a second class citizen. Jesus made her feel complete. She left with a renewed mind and confident in the person she was in Christ. She was so excited, she went into the city to tell everyone to come see the Man who made her feel better about herself. That is the feeling I want to have each and every time I have an encounter with Jesus.

I look at the women in my surroundings and I know some of the things they have gone through, so I understand many of their actions. But as I do a collective overview of their lives and mine, I've come to discover that if we as women ever fully realize and grasp hold of what God really thinks of us, then people will have no choice but to respect and admire who God has called us to be. Psalm 139:13-14 says "For you formed my inward parts; you knitted me together in my mother's womb. I praise you for I am fearfully and wonderfully made. Wonderful are your works; my soul knows it very well" (ESV). I love how this passage of scripture showed how God sees, feels, and values us as women. Once we as women began to realize this, people will be left with one of two options: they will either treat her in the way god intended or walk away to find someone else.

According to Strong's concordance the Hebrew word for fearfully is Yare (yaw-ray') which means to reverence, honor, and respect. It also means to inspire, reverence, or Godly fear/awe. The phrase 'wonderfully made' has the Greek word palah (paw-law') which means to be renowned, set apart, and different from anyone or anything else. When women view that verse with that perspective, it takes on a whole new outlook. God took out so much time in developing us and molding us into the people we are. He paid so much attention to us that we were like no other women on this earth. We are unique, invaluable, and irreplaceable. That is so amazing to me. That is one of the many reasons God requires man to hold us with the utmost respect and admiration, because that is how he sees us. If that is how God sees us, how can we dare accept anything less? God holds us in high regard so it's no wonder that He requires that man does the same.

Reading Proverbs 31 has given me even more insight on my worth and why God holds me in such high regard. It teaches me why it is so very important to wait on God to send the right person(s) into my lives. Since I've learn this about myself, I find myself telling women they need to know their worth. Once we find our worth we will be less likely to put up with many of the negative things others bring into our lives.

I find that most women look at this passage as a guideline on how we need to be for our future husband. Although that is true, I found that Proverbs 31 does not only talk about how a woman should be with her husband. It also talks about how she is with her children and the community. God will send people into our lives for various reasons and for particular seasons in life. Proverbs 31 never stated how or why people were in her life, only that she treated them with respect and she received respect in return.

When I look at the woman described in Proverbs, I discovered not only does her husband and children respect, honor, and praise her; but the whole city respects her and holds her in high regard. I love how the New Living Translation breaks down verse 29 "There are many virtuous and capable women in the world, but you surpass them all!" This scripture shows that she is a woman who has the ability to command respect as well as give respect. It also conveys that people who come in contact with her are given an understood set of choices. Their first choice is to treat her the way God intended for her to be treated. Second is to walk away and move on to the next person. Their third alternative is to stay and deal with the repercussions from God for the mistreatment of His valuable jewel. That is why it is so important that men believe the scripture, Proverbs 18:22, that when a man finds that one woman God has for him, he finds a good thing. The added bonus in him finding her is that he also gains the favor of God. I believe that when a man takes hold of that verse and truly understands that he has an important and priceless gift from God, only then can he began to see women in a whole new light. He will also know what aspects and attributes to seek when searching God for his wife.

In verse 11 of Proverbs 31, we find that a virtuous woman can be trusted by her husband because he knows and understands that she would not do anything to hurt him or the family. Part b of verse 11 states that his wife has the ability to supply for his every need. Also she is a very wise woman and knows how to invest her income in order to help provide for her family. The NCV says it this way, "Her husband trusts her completely. With her, he has everything he needs". A virtuous woman is not a compulsive person who goes out and buys things just because. She is quite the opposite; she contemplates each transaction and dealing in order to make the wisest choice. In other words, she is very prude when it comes to financial dealings."

I contemplate the role of women in our society today and what is considered to be the normal role of a woman. There are many who believe that a woman's place is at home and the husband works to provide for the family. There is absolutely nothing wrong with that and there are many who live by those standards. However what many people must understand is that being a housewife entails more than sitting at home and letting the man pay all the bills. She has to be able to find ways to support her husband, balance the finances, help in the community, and be a Godly role model for her children.

Verse 11 also takes on another meaning when it said the man has "everything" he needs. In this verse it reveals why a virtuous woman is so priceless. She provides more than monetary value to the family as well as supplies her husband support spiritually, emotionally and physically. When a man has all those aspects at home, there is no need for him to look elsewhere for anything. He has no doubt that the woman will be able to take great care of their children's needs as well as any needs that he has.

This book places great emphasis on being a virtuous woman. She should have knowledge on how to handle business affairs and how she uses her skills to profit her family. For instance in verses 16 & 17, "She inspects a field land buys it. With money SHE earned, she plants a vineyard. She does her work with energy and her arms are strong" (NCV). Clearly she is a person who does not mind working to help provide for her family.

I can hear you ask, "What about the women who have husbands who don't want them to work"? The role of a housewife is no different from a woman who has an everyday job. Even though they don't have a 9-5, they work every day. There are things that she does to make sure the home is taken care of. A true housewife is certainly not a home body, but she is one who takes on many hats to ensure the care of her family. When you look into the day of a *true* housewife you will see that she has very little time to lie around watching television all day. Just to name a few things; she has a husband to get up and see off to work, kids to get up and dressed for school, breakfast to cook, and a house to clean. In addition to that she has clothes to wash, iron, fold and put up. If she knows how to sew, she will have to mend and/or patch clothes. Considering the prospect of her having school aged children, she attends school activities, participates in the PTA, and takes on the role as a classroom mom.

A virtuous woman does not waste time on things that have no purpose. In fact, she is a woman full of purpose. In verse 27 it says she is not a lazy person, but she is always looking out for things pertaining to her family. The NCV says it this way, "She watches over her family and never wastes her time". She has no time for gossip nor is she a woman who is known for lying around doing nothing all day. Gossip can be easily put this way; if you are discussing an issue in which you are not part of the problem or the solution, then you are gossiping. She is constantly thinking of ways to better her family. Once she finds an opportunity, she considers all the pros and cons of the situation before making a final decision. She is also known as a great caretaker of her children and teaches her children how to obey and respect others.

There are a few highlights to that whole passage that I want to bring to light. For me, the main point is how she knows the correct way to be submissive. According to verses 11 & 12, "The heart of her husband safely trusts her: So he will have no lack of gain. She does him good and not evil all the days of her life (NKJV). In taking a closer look at the word submit, I find that it's not a list of rules and regulations but rather it's a state of being. We as women can have a voice, but at the end of the day, the head of the household makes the final decision. I know many women tend to think that submissiveness is being a *yes woman* but that is definitely not true. Virtuous women certainly have a mind of their own and are able to make decisions for themselves. The difference is she knows how to get her husband to listen to her without being overbearing. She can make most decisions on her own, but she is strong enough to submit to her husband and allow him to have the final say in matters. She is able to support him and allow him to be the head that God intended.

I also find in the scriptures that she has a meek and humble spirit. In verse 20 it says "She extends a helping hand to the poor and opens her arms to the needy" (NLT). To understand the meaning of humility and meekness we must first know what it means. According to the dictionary, humility is the quality or condition of being humble; lowliness, meekness, submissiveness. Meekness is patient, long-suffering, submissive in disposition or nature, humble, and gentle. I began to think on those words a pastor once said about meekness not meaning weakness. I have heard that many times but I have never listened or truly understood those words until recently.

My brothers and I were raised mainly by my mother and grandmother. My mother had to work a lot in order to support the family, so the bulk of many things fell on the shoulders of my grandmother. During my childhood, there was never a real male figure to show neither us how a woman should be treated nor one to show how a woman should treat a man. I was raised to be self-sufficient and possessed the mindset that if I didn't do it for myself it wouldn't get done. I've learned so much from reading the book of Proverbs. As you read further into this book, my goal is to show you the different aspects of a virtuous woman from the eyes of different women in the bible.

Chapter 3

SARAH: ABRAHAM'S VIRTUOUS WIFE

The first example I found is Abram's wife Sarai on her amazing ability to submit and obey her husband. Women tend to look at submission as an ugly word and think it means the woman is a "yes" girl. That can't be farther from the truth. The Greek word for submission is "hypotasso", pronounced hü-po-tä's-sō, which means to place oneself under. The Greek-English Lexicon defines it as "submission in the sense of voluntary yielding in love". All the Greek translation books liken it to being in the military. When a person joins the military, they are voluntarily placing themselves in a position where they must take orders from another person. The soldier's role is to support the leader and make every effort for the leader to have successful missions whether or not he/she likes the leader's method of carrying it out. That is how it is in being a submissive woman/wife. A wife may not like all the decisions her husband makes, but her roles are to support him and be there to uplift him when he falls.

I think about Genesis chapter 12 when Abram told his wife to lie to Pharaoh and say that she was his sister. There is no mention of her disagreeing with the decision although if she was like any female, she probably had a million things running through her head she wanted to say. She didn't say anything because she realized that Abram was following God and if he was doing wrong then it was God who would correct him. She supported his decision no matter how outlandish it may have seemed.

I think about us as women today. Would we be so willing to pretend to be our husband's "sister" just for the sake of trying to get out of trouble that does not appear real at the moment? I can imagine that we would have an argument with our spouse and say no we are not going to do it. We would take it as our husband being ashamed to own us as his wife, not as it being an attempt to save his life and risk leaving the wife alone. Yes that may seem selfish, but we have all done things for selfish reasons. In the end, the king still found out the truth because God placed a curse on the land. The Pharaoh questioned Abram's actions and ended up letting he and his wife go without inflicting harm. So although Sarai didn't say anything, God still had her in mind and handled the situation.

Another thing I admire about Sarai is that she doesn't have the "I told you so" mentality. Later in Genesis, God changed Abram and Sarai names to Abraham and Sarah. One would think that Abraham learned his lesson on lying from his first experience with a king. But you will see Abraham make the same mistake in Genesis Chapter 20. Abraham and Sarah go into the region of Negev where Abimelik is King. Abraham, once again, decided to deceive the king by saying that Sarah was his sister. I laughed here because I think about women of today and their immediate reaction. Once again, you will not read anywhere where Sarah said anything in disagreement to her husband. There was no bring up the past, no telling him she was not going to do it, nor was there any downgrading him because of the request he made. In fact, Sarah knew that it was a possibility that she would have to sleep with another man in order to uphold the story that Abraham had told, yet there is no mention where she even said a word of disagreement. So can you, as a woman, imagine holding your peace when you know that your husband is doing wrong and you know the consequences of the actions taken? Those thoughts had to be going through Abraham's mind also, but he was looking at the immediate threat and not really concerning himself with the future consequences. So the underlying question is: did he trust his wife enough to know that she wouldn't allow anything like that to happen? That brings to mind Proverbs 31:11-12 "Her husband trusts her completely. With her, he has everything he needs. She does him good and not harm for as long as she lives" (NCV).

Sarah is a prime example of how a woman can still have flaws, yet still be that virtuous woman that God has called. She talked her husband into sleeping with another woman resulting in the woman becoming pregnant. After the woman had the baby, she became jealous and talked Abraham into sending the woman and her son away. She laughed at the angel when she was told she was going to have a baby. Lastly, she then lied to the angel by saying she didn't laugh. In all that, God still blessed her and her husband and allowed them to be the seed of many generations to come. Her husband is known as the father of faith. Her son would continue the legacy that his mother and father began.

Chapter 4

RAHAB: THE UNSUNG VIRTUOUS WOMAN

The next woman that I would consider virtuous is Rahab. I know many wonder, how is it possible for Rahab to be considered virtuous? She was a well-known prostitute. As I was reading the book of Joshua, I began to see how Rahab paid attention to the move of God because she told the spies of the things God had already done to the enemies of the Israelites. I pray that as you read this section you will gain understanding and insight into the life of Rahab and learn how she became virtuous. We have to realize that virtuous women are not born, they are developed. It is learned and it is very important that we obtain wisdom on how to become one. Only then can we obtain God's very best for our lives. Because Rahab was well-known as a prostitute, many doubted her potential and insight. She saw the hand of God moving, knew the city was going to be destroyed, and decided to protect the spies who came to scout out the land.

I really can't help but admire Rahab for her courage in hiding the spies. She took a risk that many of us would probably have not had the strength to do. She took a huge risk in hiding the spies and lying to the men whom the king sent to retrieve from her home. Her very actions caused her to be listed in the book of James and Hebrew as a woman of faith. James 2:25 says "In the same way, was not even Rahab the prostitute considered righteous for what she did when she gave lodging to the spies and sent them off in a different direction" (NIV). Hebrews 11:31 tells us "By faith Rahab the harlot did not perish along with those who were disobedient, after she had welcomed the spies in peace" (NASB).

What makes her virtuous you ask? We can go back to the primary scripture of Proverbs and look at verse 26 & 27 "When she speaks, her words are wise, and kindness is the rule for everything she says. She watches carefully all that goes on throughout her household and is never lazy" (TLB). So in protecting the spies she gained favor in God's eyes. She was wise enough to know that a change was coming and she didn't want to be left behind. She also ensured that her family was not destroyed in the battle. The spies took into account that she helped them and made the promise that everyone in her household would be spared as long as they were in her home under her protection. Her family respected and trusted her enough to stay home during the battle. Rahab realized the town's people were judging her based on her reputation; however she used wisdom given to her in order to deceive them. Because of her obedience and her willingness to help, she and all her family were spared from a tragic end. Not only that, she became part of the linage of Jesus by marrying Salmon, a prince of the house of Judah, and giving birth to Boaz. Boaz would end up marrying the next virtuous woman indicated in chapter five.

Chapter 5

RUTH: THE SINGLE AND VIRTUOUS WOMAN

Ruth is a very well –known woman of the Bible. There are so many women who refer to this scripture when asking God for a mate. They are eager for their "Boaz" to find them. But we all must ask ourselves a very important question: Are we willing to do what Ruth did in order for our Boaz to find us? Ruth endured many things before she was able to be with the man God had for her. When God took me to this book I really didn't want to read it. I thought God was trying to prepare me for a mate and I was nowhere near the point of wanting a Boaz in my life. I told God I was content with the fact that I needed to learn more about myself and what He needed me to do in life. But God wouldn't let me go anywhere else but the book of Ruth. So I finally settled in to see what God wanted me to learn from Ruth and I was amazed at what was revealed to me in this book.

Studying the book of Ruth showed me there is so much more in there than just the coming together of Ruth and Boaz. It was more than having someone who is there to protect and to provide. It deals with trust, submission, and obedience in order for God to develop and mature Ruth to become the virtuous woman Boaz needed in his life. The first part I want to cover is trust. Ruth was given every opportunity to leave Naomi after Naomi lost her husband and all her sons, but she chose to stay with Naomi and continue to serve Naomi's God. I still sit back and wonder would I have done the same thing as Ruth when she chose to follow her mother-in-law.

I've talked with various married women and ask about their relationship with their in-laws. More often than not, they say that the relationship is scarce if not non-existent. I think about the relationship I had with my mother-in-law before and after my divorce. We had a great relationship where we would sit and talk on the phone for hours. She was not one who cooked often but when I would come into town she would make sure she cooked whatever I requested.

When I began studying this chapter, my mother-in-law passed away just months before. I asked myself if she were to leave and go to another state or country, would I have been willing to drop everything I had and followed. My answer was always no, I would not be willing.

Although I loved her dearly, I didn't trust her enough to leave my home and family to go to an unknown place and start a new life. Ruth showed unwavering devotion to her mother-in-law and trusted Naomi to the point where she denounced her gods in order to follow Naomi's God. How many of us would have done as Ruth and have been willing to give up everything we knew only to find there was better in store.

The second thing I'd like to bring out was that Ruth was first submissive to her mother-in-law. Submission does not always pertain to male authority. It can be anyone who is in authority or someone who is wiser than us. Because of her close relationship with Naomi, Ruth understood the wisdom of Naomi and was willing to submit herself to Naomi's teaching and guidance. When reading the book of Ruth, we see that not once did Ruth object to anything Naomi asked of her. She subjected herself to possible humiliation by obeying the things Naomi told her to do. I think of Ruth and how it compares to us as women of today. Today there is so little respect for our elderly women. They are so full of wisdom and if we would sit and listen to some things, we would come out a lot wiser. I look at one act in particular. Naomi asked Ruth to go and lay at the feet of Boaz. During that timeframe, it was a huge risk for Ruth. She was running the risk of Boaz rejecting her. But custom was that if a woman was widowed and left childless, she could not marry outside the family. The nearest relative was to marry her and the firstborn son would carry the dead husband's name so that his name would not be blotted out (Deuteronomy 25:5-10). Ruth was advised to uncover Boaz's feet and lay there letting him know that he was the next in line to marry her and help in carrying on her husband's name.

There is also another type of submission of Ruth and that was submission to Boaz even before he claimed her as wife. When Boaz rolled over in the middle of the night and saw her, she immediately told him who she was and for him to cover her. That in itself shows an aspect in Ruth that we as women of today could learn. Boaz noticed it and commended her on her actions by saying in verses 10-11"Blessed are you of the Lord, my daughter! For you have shown more kindness at the end than at the beginning, in that you did not go after young men, whether poor or rich. And now, my daughter, do not fear. I will do for you all that you request, for all the people of my town know that you are a virtuous woman" (NKJV). That statement alone demonstrated that Boaz had been watching the actions of Ruth the entire time. He noticed that she was not a haughty person, mean, nor did she think she deserved anything for free. She worked for what she obtained. She had some independence but she knew when to submit and listen to others. By being humble and obedient to God, she married Boaz and became part of the linage of Jesus.

Chapter 6

HANNAH: ELKANAH'S VIRTUOUS WIFE

This section will talk about my absolute favorite woman of the bible. 1 Samuel talks about Hannah and the things she had to go through before getting to God's promise. She is one that, I feel, is the epitome of what a virtuous woman should be. She was a humble, wise, and obedient. She never complained, grumbled, nor was she vindictive during her ordeal. She endured ridicule, misunderstanding, and low self-esteem issues. She continued to believe God and his promise even when things were at their worst.

I look at how she handled the situation with Peninnah, Elkanah's second wife, and I have to admire the grace in which she took the ridicule. Peninnah mocked Hannah for not being able to have children, yet Hannah never tried to retaliate nor told her husband how she was being treated. I sometimes wonder if Peninnah ever saw the effect that she had on Hannah and continued to make mockery simply because she took pleasure in Hannah's pain. Some people may think it was weak for Hannah not to say or do anything to Peninnah. I say it shows her inner strength and perseverance because it was considered a curse from God if a woman was not able to conceive children during this time in history. It was also thought that the woman had not gained favor with God if she didn't have a male child to carry on the father's name. Peninnah never let Hannah forget these facts about her situation.

The Holman Christian Standard Bible calls Peninnah Hannah's rival which in the Greek means antípalos. Antípalos means someone who is competing with another with the same goal in mind or for superiority in the same area of activity. Webster dictionary puts it this way: "One who is in pursuit of the same object as another; one striving to reach or obtain something which another is attempting to obtain, and which one only can possess". Iit is very possible Peninnah felt threatened by Hannah. She wanted the same love and attention that Elkanah showed Hannah to be shown to her. She saw that Elkanah favored Hannah over her and she knew that affection could only deepen if Hannah were to have a child.

Hannah handled everything Peninnah threw at her with such humility and grace. She never complained to God about Peninnah.

She never asked God to avenge her. Though knowing that people thought she was cursed, Hannah never once questioned God on why she never had children. She didn't allow bitterness to set in towards Peninnah, her husband, or God. All she knew was that she needed to pour her heart out to God. She confessed her brokenness and pledge to dedicate her child back to God if He would bless her with one.

You can tell that Hannah never told her husband anything that was going on because he was clueless as to why she was sad every year. In 1 Samuel 1:8, it shows how Elkanah would ask Hannah what was wrong and why she was not eating. He was thinking that it was because she did not have any sons. It didn't dawn on him that Peninnah was taunting Hannah because of her infertility. To see how her husband spoiled her by giving her a double portion of the meat for sacrifice to Hannah shows that he completely loved and trusted her. He understood the part in Proverbs where it says her value is far more than that of any jewelry and he truly treated her like she was a priceless ruby. Although he didn't truly understand all that Hannah was going through; he could still see and feel her pain and wanted to do whatever was in his power to alleviate that pain. This demonstrates that he was a man who paid attention to his wife and knew when things were not right with her.

It is easy to see she suffered from depression. The Bible states that when she was ridiculed by Peninnah she would cry and would not eat. Each year it came time to go to the Lord's house she would look downcast and dejected. She is known because her husband asked her about why she was crying and not eating. Her anguish even showed in her praying. The priest came to her to ask her what was wrong and thought she was intoxicated. Even during this time, she would not do anything that would discredit the person she was.

Hannah was also a good judge of character. Hannah has an ability to know who to trust and talk to when she had a crisis. Women are well known to be gossips when the bible clearly states that gossiping should not be one of our characteristics. Proverbs 31 describes how a virtuous woman does not engage in gossip. In fact it tells us that women are to speak with wisdom and kindness. You will also see that the bible never tells us that Hannah went to any other person about the things she was going through. There was no meeting up with her female friends to talk about her personal issues. Hannah went to the tabernacle and poured her heart out to God. She knew that God was the only one who was able to do anything about her situation.

When Hannah went to the tabernacle to pray, she made a vow saying that if God would only allow her to give birth to a male child, she would dedicate that child back to God and would never cut his hair. During this prayer the priest saw her and thought she was drunk. When the priest came to her, she never acted out of character. She only told the priest there was something troubling her and that she was talking to God about her situation. In her agony, she still didn't tell the priest what she was going through; instead she kept that between her and God. When the priest saw her heart and knew she was sincere in what she said, he prayed that God would grant whatever she requested. After her time of prayer and encounter with Eli, she left so uplifted that she went home and ate.

Final thoughts on Hannah are the fact that she would still remain faithful to God whether He blessed her with a child or not. The Lord did honor her request and she kept her vow to God. Proverbs 31:30 encourages us to praise a woman who reverences God and that we should give her what's due. How much more will God do for a virtuous woman? God heard Hannah's request so when she slept with her husband the next night, she conceived and later gave birth to a baby boy. After the baby was weaned Hannah kept her word and took the baby back to the tabernacle to be given back to God. This is so profound how Elkanah trusted his wife so much that he never once told her she could not do it. The only thing he told her was to do as she saw fit and his only requirement was that that the child be established in God's word. Can you imagine giving your baby to someone and only seeing them once a year? As a result of her faithfulness, God honored her and opened her womb. Samuel 2:21 goes on later to inform us that Hannah had 3 sons and 2 daughters. This truly brings home the last verse in Proverb 31, "Give her of the fruit of her hands, and let her own works praise her in the gate [of the city]!" (AMP). Hannah is a true example of a virtuous woman.

Chapter 7

TODAY'S VIRTUOUS WOMEN

This section is dedicated to the women who have had an impact on my life and the lives of people around me. I did a post on Facebook a while back and asked what my friends thought a virtuous woman should be. There were a few answers but one pulled me to the side after church and said that there was no way a woman can be virtuous like the women in the bible. That comment took me for a loop and I began to think about why a person would have such thoughts. I asked her why did she think that way and she told me that the women of the bible had very different roles than the women of today and what was done back then are not the same things done today. So this book really originated because I wanted to see what the major differences were in the women of the bible verses the women of today. As I looked and studied I realized there was not much difference as far as how we are to be as women. The roles may have changed but the concept of being virtuous is still the same.

I've spoken with a couple of women in which I would like to highlight in this chapter. The first woman is someone I met through a church impact group and became dear friends. We laugh now, but when we first met my words to her were "if I don't learn anything in this group I will not ever be back". She just smiled and said she understood and hoped that I would get something out of our gatherings. Since that day I've learned so much from her and how to be able to have a closer relationship with not only Christ, but also with people. As I talk about her further, I am taking into context Proverbs 31 where virtuous women open their arms to those less fortunate, how they have strength and dignity, and how they speak with wisdom and instructions.

I looked at how my friend would pray with others, answer calls at all times of the night, or even leave home during the night just to go pray with someone. Many women look up to her for advice and direction. There has never been a time where I've known her to turn anyone away.

It amazes me because she seems to effortlessly manage everything. She is the mother of three daughters and the grandmother of one grandson. One of her daughters passed away a few years ago and even through that she was able to minister and help others. I can recollect an event where I called her right after her daughter died and asked her how she could possibly smile and continue when her daughter was gone. Her response to me was that it was Jesus giving her strength and that she realized that there was a greater plan in store for her. She also said that her pain would become part of her ministry. All I could say was I just pray that God never tested me that way, but I learned there was strength in adversity no matter what it was you're going through.

I went to her house last year and we talked about the importance of being single and virtuous. I asked her what her thoughts were on dating and being submissive to someone who was not yet your husband. She thought about it for a minute then she said that when a person is dating, it should not be for a pastime but is should be for the purpose of being with the man God intended for you marry. She also stated when it comes to being submissive, there are some things a single woman should not do when dating. The main thing single women should not do is share their bodies with someone who is not their husband. If the man is not willing to wait, then that is the perfect sign that he is not the one for you. The second most important thing is that if the relationship is new or if you see that it is not going anywhere, you should not be giving your financial information to him. She also talked about how being submissive to your mate exactly relates to how you are submissive to your church leadership. If you are not willing to follow your pastor when you are single, how can you follow the man God has planned to place in your life as your mate?

I was also aware of how her daughters respected what she said and how they also knew how to worship without a care of who was watching. In this same session, I spoke with her youngest daughter on what things she valued most about her mom. Her response was that she admired how her mom worshiped God no matter where she was. She also talked about how her mom began teaching them at an early age on how to worship and have their own relationship with God. I asked her about her thoughts on her mother's rules about dating. She stated that she didn't always agree with what her mother says, but she respects her mother's decision because she knows that her mother's decision were based off wisdom and was in place to keep her safe. That very statement took me back to Proverbs 31. A virtuous woman has children who call her blessed.

The next woman I would like to highlight is the first lady of my church. Although we have known each other for years, I never really got to know her until she married my pastor. I've always thought she was a woman who never said much and would agree with anything. I now know that she is a strong opinionated woman with vision and purpose. I've watched through the years I see where she is full of wisdom and knowledge. She is very supportive of the things her husband does and if there was any disruption in the home, you never knew anything about it. She reminds me so much of Hannah in that she keeps things and prays about it instead of talking about it. I see how her husband ALWAYS talks about her on Sundays. He's not ashamed of the fact that he loves her unconditionally and how he trusts her with his whole being. If you remember, Proverbs 31 explains about how a man has complete trust in his wife and he lacks nothing with her. I've come to see how the young women of the church look to her for guidance and direction. She is one that corrects with love. She sits, explains, and helps come up with a plans to get back on track. I even see how her children highly respect her and her daughter is learning at a very young age how to become a virtuous woman after God's heart.

I have another friend whom I met in college. I didn't know how valuable she would be as a friend. We laugh a lot because our daughters are two days apart. Even back before we had kids she showed signs of a virtuous woman. We don't get to talk as much as we used to but when we do, it's just like we talked yesterday. I take a look now at how she raises her kids and attends to her husband. I absolutely love her kids. I had the pleasure of sitting with them one day and I just had to sit back and smile at how much they respect her. She has also taken my daughter under her wing. My daughter adores her and is always asking to go over to stay. I know I can trust her because I see how she loves and protects her own. She is very careful of what her children watch and that they are exposed. That shows how much she attends to the care and well-being of her children.

The last woman that I would like to highlight is my mother. Although we have not always agreed on everything, my mother has always been a constant rock in my life. I grew up watching her serve the community. Whenever someone called, she did her best to meet whatever need there was at the time. I can remember always going to church and wondering why we had to be there every single Sunday for every single service. We not only attended church service at our home church, but my mother would take us to visit other churches on Sunday. We knew that Sundays meant attending church all day. She raised us to always be nice to everyone because you never knew when we would have to be in that same situation. I never really understood that back then, but I fully understand her teachings now.

My brothers and I would not dare to disrespect my mother or anyone else. There were always consequences to our actions, but she always tried to discipline in love. Even now I respect my mom just as much as I did growing up if not more. I can remember nights where I would wake up in the middle of the night and see my mom on her knees praying. There was never a night that I didn't see my mom sitting in the bed reading her bible before going to sleep. When we would go to prayer meeting, she would be one of the women of the church who always prayed. I laugh now, but I thought it was so embarrassing back then on how people would always call on her to give the answers to hard bible study questions. I preferred for them to call on someone other than my mom because that would mean they thought I should know the answers too.

The thing that really showed me how people admired and called her blessed was when we had her surprise birthday party. There were people there from our community and as well as neighboring town. There were so many people who attended that we ran out of room in the facility. Many who couldn't come made sure I knew they were not coming but to let my mom know they were thinking about her. It warmed my heart to know that so many people thought well of her. It was also good for her to see that people appreciated the work that she had done in and around our community. I think her biggest surprise was to see that family who flew in and rode trains to be there for that day. Many left that next day but for them to come and stay for that one day did her heart well. Those actions alone remind me of the last verse in Proverbs 31 which states "give her of the fruit of her hands; and let her own works praise her in the gates" (KJV). My mother continues to teach us a lot and she is also still very active in our community.

Chapter 8

CONCLUSION

I hope that you have enjoyed and learned as much as I have on how to be a virtuous woman. Being virtuous does not mean being perfect. For instance, Sarah made bad judgment calls but she still found favor with God. Rahab was a prostitute, but she learned how to turn things around and obey the voice of God. Hannah neglected to let her husband know what was really going on, but she still found a way to get in touch with God. My friends that I spoke about are not perfect, but they love God with all their heart. They strive every day to be more like Christ. We all have our flaws and failures that we deal with on a regular basis. What sets us apart is how we deal with the flaws and failures. We have to know that God's purpose and plan must be done and that we are to do our part to teach and do for others.

No matter what your background, you can always learn to be the woman God intended for you to be. It does not matter if you have been abused physically, mentally, or emotionally you can still become a virtuous woman. God loves you with everything He has. He loved women so much that he made us last as a gift to man. When you realize your identity and value in Christ only then can you evolve into this woman of virtue. It does not happen overnight. You must continue to persevere even when it seems that things are at their worst. Trust and know that God's very best for you will be the result.

Acknowledgements

First I want to thank God for using me to put on paper what has been placed into my heart. I want to say thank you to my mom for always giving love and support throughout the years. Thank you to my Pastor and first lady Robert and Angela Johnson. The two of you have been a constant rock that I can depend on to pray me through things and always show love and support. Much love to my friends Tanya, Sal, Renita, Valerie, and Leanna. You guys have been there from the very beginning. Thank you all for all the love and support you gave, for the encouraging words and believing in me when I didn't believe for myself. And last but certainly not least a shout out to my Real Life Church family. You all have been so very supportive and it has not gone unnoticed.

About the Author

S onia Williams is a native of a small town in Jayess, MS. She graduated from the University of Southern Mississippi with a bachelors in Psychology. In her spare time she loves to write and spend time with family.

Printed in the United States
By Bookmasters